Emojicode Programming for Parents

Teach your Children Programming Basics in 30 Days or Less Using Emojis

Table of Contents

Introduction

Congratulations on purchasing *Emojicode Programming for Parents*.

Wow, is this the book that you have been waiting for, or what? So many kids are playing on laptops, phones, and gaming systems these days, that it is no surprise that Emojicode has become a new language for coding. This generation of kids always tries to find a new way to advance his or her knowledge and learning to code is one way to contribute to expanding their knowledge base. With the advancement in technology and increase in curiosity in children, it has become important for children to learn to code. Children have started to code at the age of five and to cater to their needs, the world has developed a language called Emojicode, which is a programming language that uses emoticons to derive the required output. In fact, some of the most influential leaders in computer programming are starting their careers as young as 20.

The Emojicode was developed when the developer had to decode a message a friend had sent to him. This message was riddled with emojis and made it difficult for the developer to understand what the message was. When he thought about it, he realized that people across the globe used emoticons to express their thoughts and emotions. He then decided to develop a code that used emoticons. The Emojicode was developed in the year 2016, and now it is taking the world by storm. Are you ready to jump on the bandwagon and begin coding your heart out?

The book discusses all the information you need to gather to begin coding using Emojicode. Use Emojicode to help you design programs and games that can be fun and useful without the need to learn harder programming languages, such as HTML, CSS, or C++. You can use Emojicode on your Mac or Windows Computer and the best thing about the code is that it is simple, thereby making it easy for kids to understand. If you follow the syntax and code mentioned in the book, you can develop your first game by tomorrow!

There are plenty of books on this subject in the market, and thanks again for choosing this one! Every effort has been made to ensure it is packed with as much useful information as possible, please enjoy!

Chapter One
An Introduction to Emojicode

(Emojicode website: https://www.emojicode.org/)

What is Emojicode?

Computer coding has intrigued not only adults but kids too. Ever since the onset of the computer generation, kids have only grown up with technology. They use tablets, computers, or cell phones regularly and are adept at technology when compared to older generations. It is no wonder that we see computer programmers starting out young and creating their digital footprint in the industry. Due to the new age demographics, there are more and more young people who utilize computer programming regularly.

Emojicode is a language that kids often use to not only communicate with each other but to also communicate with their parents.

Emojicode is bridging the gap between the young and the old in a fun new way. It is a form of computer programming that allows the programmer to use emojis to write a code. This language is used by those who want to create simple programs and games. Emojicode is a modern and powerful feature that makes writing programs easy. It also makes it a fun way to write codes. There are classes and optionals that can handle the absence of value, closures, generics, and a list of texts.

This code is strongly typed meaning that the compiler can verify if all the operations in the code are correct. This type of language can help with multiple things including ensuring that the numbers in the code are not treated as text.

Emojicode has a structure that is similar to the programming language C. The only difference is that we use emojis to write the code instead of text. Emojicode was developed to allow for the development of a platforms applications independence. They accomplish this by running the code through a virtual machine.

The code is first broken down into bytecode by the compiler and is then executed. This process is called Emojicode Real-time and it helps to execute your code faster. It is the implementation reference for the virtual machine.

Emojicode is not the first novelty coding program to hit the internet; in fact, there have been several coding programs developed with the purpose of only writing prose in Shakespearean language, the rhetoric of the one and only Donald Trump, and even a code designed to give instructions on how to perform card tricks.

Emojicode was started as a GitHub project and has only been in the market for a few years, but it is popular among the teens because of its uniqueness. Emojicode, although a novel language, features a compiler that deals strictly with Emojicode and an execution engine that is solely designed for Emojicode. The steps taken are simple - Emojicode programming is reduced to Emojicode bytecode, the bytecode is run in the compiler environment after which it is virtualized.

Emojicode is developed to work in its own package management system, which will allow those that are developers of Emojicode to create a useful tool in order to use the language. The packages that will come bundled with the Emojicode include one for a navigation file and another that allows for interacting within the SQL database. If you download new packages, you will improve the functionality of the language.

One thing that should be noted is that Emojicode is not written completely in emojis. For example, variable names are not written as emojis. To write the program, you must use normal text. However, there are some inbuilt programs that are referenced with emojis. Methods, which are modular units of code that perform a specific function, are often referenced with emojis. Another example is the data type which can be integers, strings, and characters to name only a few. Classes are also only written as emojis since they can be referenced in another section of the code or in a different code.

Several parts of the program use emojis. These parts often include the variables that are used to execute the program. For instance, a tiny bearded face can be used to demarcate the comments. Comments help another user understand what the output of a section of code will be. They cannot be compiled or executed. Boolean operators, the true and false functions, are referenced as the thumbs up and thumbs down emojis. The conditional statements can be represented with orange slices.

The Emojicode was developed by Theo Weidman when he realized that emoticons can be used to send messages to people. He simply wanted to create text that could be used to communicate. However, he developed a programming language that only had emojis. Classes were developed at the initial stage, but the protocols and other intricate details were developed much later. He did not want the NULL value to pop up when the code was not written correctly. Instead, he chose to develop optionals as well as closures.

Hello, World in Emojicode:

How is it Used?

Now that we have learned a little more about Emojicode, let us spend some time to understand how the language is used. Since its inception, the language has provided an easier way to focus on the integration of systems and its compatibility with Unicode, thereby providing a stable and consistent interface.

When Can You Use It?

Emojicode is best used whenever you wish to use it. Because of its versatility within the programming field, you can use Emojicode to create virtually anything. Since this book is designed to help kids learn how to use Emojicode to create Emojis, games, as well as programs, then knowing when to use it is quite simple. Once you download the Emojicode program into your Linux or Mac OS system you can start to use the Emojicode instantly. This book has more than enough information in it to help you know how to create the simple items we discuss in the first sections of this book. We have also given you a simple program that you can design with a step-by-step process and a game to create called Cookie Monster. Each one of these steps is self-explanatory and super easy. I will walk you through each step explaining the process and what you need to do. I also explain why you need to do those actions and what each emoji or bit of code means, and how it translates into the bits and pieces that are needed to program with emojis.

When to Use Emojis

There is sometimes a bit of confusion for when emojis can be used. They are very simple guidelines, which is within all types, initializers, and methods with the names of the emojis. Then, there is a variable which cannot involve any of the emojis, however, they need to have a combination of characters which cannot be confused with numbers.

By knowing this you can see why using an Emojicode programming system is something that can be used whenever you want. Although this is not a complete guidebook for every use of the Emojicode Programming platform, it is comprehensive enough to teach you how to use the codes with anything you would like to do within your day.

Downloading the application is super easy and installation is a breeze. The most challenging part of the Emojicode Programming system is figuring out what you want to use it on.

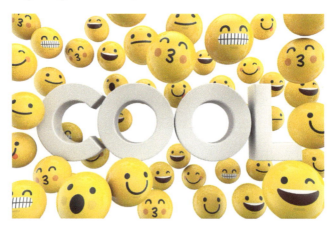

Chapter Two
Installing Emojicode

It is recommended that you use the magic installation process to install Emojicode on your system.

Magic Installation

Emojicode is one of the easiest programming languages to install, and the magic installation method is the easiest to use. You start by selecting the operating system that you are currently using and then the version of the software you need to install from a list of available options. Once you have made your selections, you can copy the commands mentioned below into a shell. This will download the script and then appropriate the Emojicode with SDK and then run the installer.

The installer will then check with you where you would like to install Emojicode. The default location would be within the /user/local/bin as well as the /user/local/EmojicodePackages. In the event that the user does not have access to those directories with the installer, the installer may suggest that you use Sudo.

Those that use Windows 10 can use the Bash on Ubuntu on the Windows 10 platform for installing and using Emojicode. At this point, you must simply click on Linux, which is the OS. The next step is to proceed with the steps that were laid out above.

Manual Installation

To install the software manually, follow the steps below:

1. Download the SDK for your system and extract the .tar file. *tar-xzf Emojicode-VERSION-YOUR-PLATFORM.tar.g*

2. Next, run the *cd Emojicode-VERSION-YOUR-PLATFORM./ install.sh* file.

In the event that your system is not already prepared to display emojis, then you will most likely have to install the ttf-ancient-fonts on the Linux platform using the following script: sudo apt-get install ttf-ancient-fonts.

If you use a Mac OS X, it is easy to display the emojis. The GitHub repository will help you with instructions that will help you build the Emojicode from your source.

Installing on Windows

With a windows system, you need to use a secondary program to run the program like Ubuntu or BASH. Both these programs can be located in the app store for Microsoft. Ubuntu is an operating system that is similar to DOS and allows you to run programs that are not windows based.

Installing on a Mac OS

This is the same process that was discussed earlier in the book. If you go to the website, select your computer version, and the system that you are using to download the program, you can download the correct version of Emojicode for your system.

Input Methods

Emojicode is a fun and easy to use programming software that will help you write fun programs. Unfortunately, the keyboard is not designed to input this code into your programming or word docs. However, there are multiple shortcuts that you can use to input these emojis into your system.

Below is a breakdown of these shortcuts that will allow us to input the Emojicode into your programming and documents. First, we will start by identifying the Mac OS shortcuts.

Mac OS Emojipicker

Entering your emojis on the Mac OS system is easy. It is as simple and easy as riding a bike. All you need to do is press the $^\wedge\mathcal{H}$ along with the space bar. This activates the emoji dialogue box from where you can select the emojis you need to use for the code. Then, you can drag it to open it into a window allowing you to have easier access to the code.

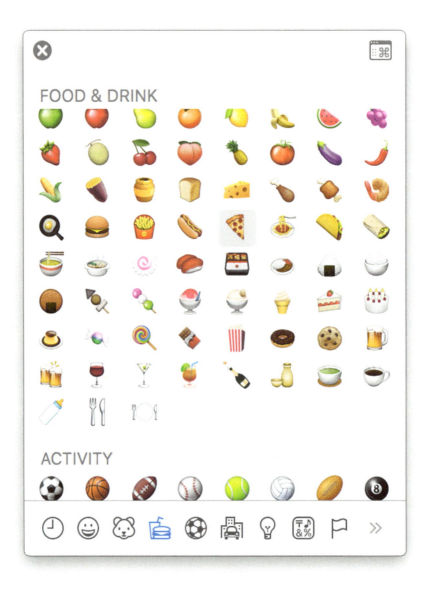

Editor Syntaxes

To write Emojicode within your favorite type of editor you can use syntax bundles and files. There are several available on the internet, but the Emojicode TextMate Bundle and Emojicode Sublime Syntax are most recommended to use.

IBus

The IBus is another style of an editor that is available for Linux/ GNU as well as the nix-like OSes. When this input method is configured correctly it should let you switch back and forth between Emojis and other applications that you may be working with.

Compose (Hex code)

The hex code is fairly user-friendly, but it may give off a bit of a hacky feel to you. All you have to do is hit the *ctrl+shift+u* keys and then using the hex codes for the specific emoji, type the hex code in and press enter.

Run-Time Native Linking

When you start up the program and load it, your Real-Time Engine will dynamically load all the static libraries which basically link all the methods for your package within the corresponding function within the dynamic library. There should be a sort of linking table which is simply a function of long lists. Within the Real-Time Engine, you can link all the functions by simply looking in the index that is provided with a 📻 within the declaration method.

Later in this book, you will read more about this subject. This is a procedure that is called *Run-Time Native Linking*.

API

Emojicode has an API that provides basic access to details like code point, name, image, and description. However, it is important to remember that the access to the API is only provided on a case-to-case basis and the applications for access are closed. You can check with the developers on Github about the access to the API.

Retaining Objects

Since there are 2 Thread Methods that are important for the releasing and retaining of objects.

```
RetainedObjectPointer retain (Object
              *object);
       void release (int n);
```

In order to retain the object, you must pass it to the retain. For example:

```
auto co = thread->retain (newArray (sizeof
       (EmojicodeChar)));
```

This implements -> operator which you should use if it was a pointer object. Note this while the RetainerObjectPointer stays valid itself, and the pointers that you receive will be values with the inside of these objects that it will point to. For example:

co->val<EmojicodeChar> () which cannot stay valid within the cycles of the Garbage Collector. After performing your GCIA you must retrieve the retained pointers. At the point where you are no longer in need of the objects that you called forth, you must type the code that releases them.

```
release:
```

```
thread->release (1);
```

Releasing and retaining works similar to a stack, which means the previous object that was retained has to be released when you call out the *release*. You can release multiples of the retained objects that you have used all at once by calling the *release* with the specific number of objects that you want to release.

Compiling the Package

A good starting point is to initialize the *undefined dynamic lookup*, which is located only in Mac OS, this should not be in any other OS.

```
g++ -03 -std=c++14 -fPIC -c your
package.co -o your package.o c++ -shared
 -fPIC -undefined dynamic lookup your
      package.o -o your_package.so
```

In the event that you are accustomed to using a build system similar to CMake, you will also need to know how to check out the way the package files are being built within the Emojicode main repositories platform.

Deinitialization

In many cases, you will have certain resources that will require that they are freed up when no longer in use. It is desirable in order to free or ensure that said resource is freed when the Garbage Collector has initialized to abandon the object. Registering an object for deinitialization is best used with this functionality:

```
void registerForDeinitialization (Object
              *object);
```

This will provide a de-initializer for the object within that class.

```
(set klass-.deinit in prepareClass).
```

If you are de-initializing the object this should only be a viable option to fall back on since there is no guarantee of the garbage collector ever triggering during the time the program is run.

Marking

You must also set up the appropriate functions for marking in order to store the object pointers in a viable value area. Then, set the market functions for your class after assigning its *mark* member for the variables function.

You must also write a marker function that is proper wherein your class store will reference the objects within the area value. That marker becomes a function which is labeled within the garbage collector when they are inspecting objects and then copies that info into the new memory location. This should and must call out the functions that are appropriate for members of the mark family which correlates with every object's reference.

The mark functions:

```
    void mark(Object **of) ;
void markValueReference (Value
        **valuePointer) ;
    void markBox(Box *box) ;
```

Mark must be what is used when you have to store an object pointer that is simple. Past this is a pointer which is actually the memory location. You must also call in the *markValueReference* for the store references to the instance of the value type, and then pass the pointer to what would have the stored references. As a reference, you should be aware that this is not necessary unless the references have addressed the value types. This, however, is an unlikely situation should you ever have to deal with within the Emojicode.

Lastly, you must call in the *markBox*, which when used with a pointer you can identify the box that is marked. This becomes necessary since the box which stores the content in a remote area is the container for the value type that the box has kept the object which is being referenced by itself.

Chapter Three
Emojicode Language Basics

Types and Namespaces

Namespaces

When a type is defined, it is loaded into a namespace. The defined type can be accessed by the programmer, however, is a part of the namespace.

The type for every variable must be defined and this type can be accessed by the programmer within the namespace. Since you do not specify the type explicitly in the namespace, the compiler knows that it can access that type from the namespace when it executes the code. Alternatively, if you have not specified a type, the default namespace ● is assigned to the type. You can also specify explicitly the namespace with which you wish the namespace accessor to be:

◆ namespace name
namespace → emoji
name → emoji

This identifies the type of name the namespace will contain.

This is a great example of referring explicitly to the 🔤 class in ●:

You can only use the syntax above if you are sure of the type you want to refer to. The simple example that is listed below will declare the class 🎁 and defines that the class must be present in the namespace 🎅:

🍋|

You must remember that the class's name should nevertheless be just 🎁 however, the type should be reachable within the 🎅 namespace.

These play a very important role when trying to import packages. It is also important to note that the name of the namespace is always an emoji.

Comments

To include non-executable text into the code that you are marking as a comment. Comments start with 💀 and then the end line will break.

Example:

💬 This will end the comment at the lines end. Which is exactly here.

Comments with multiline start with the 💬🔜 and then end with the 🔚💬 which can contain the breaks in the line.

Example:

💬🔜 This is a multiline comment. You can even make

line breaks. 🔚💬

Blocks

The block is an essential part of an Emojicode Program. This block is the section of the code that is executed when it is first started.

> 💬 Get things up and running here...

An integer can also be returned in the block which can then be used to exit the code.

> 💬 Get things up and running here...
>
> ↩ 0 Return a code here.

Generics for Emojicode

Generics allow the programmer to write code where he or she can use placeholders as variable names. When this section of code is called upon by the compiler, the real variable types are called upon and used. This helps the user avoid duplication.

The following example stores objects only of a specified type. The symbol 'T' is used inside the class as a type. This symbol ensures that only specified data types can be used as arguments for the parameter.

🎉 something T 🍇

    ↩ something

🍉

🍉

Scoping

Variables can only be accessible from within the scope of where they were declared. Every block that is coded can be everything within 🍇 and 🍉 which defines a separate scope, which will disappear once the block has already been executed.

🏁 🍇

🍦 work 🔤Work It Harder Make It Better🔤

🍉👆🍇

😀 work 💀 work is accessible here

🍦 doIt 🔤Do It Faster, Makes Us Stronger🔤

🍉

😀 work 💀 work still works, of course

😀 doIt 💀 doIt is no longer accessible here

🍉

You cannot access the scopes beyond the initializers or methods in your code. However, you can access the scope object within the instances of initializers and methods. Closures can be considered the exceptions from this very rule. You will obtain the knowledge that is needed for the two kinds of special scopes within the value and classes types, as well as the callable.

Literals

Numeric Literals

The integer of the literals will be written in:

- A notation of decimals similar to 0.**29**

- A notation of hexadecimal that is set with the prefix of **0x** similar to **0x1d**

- A notation of octal that is set with the prefix of **0** similar to **035**.

You can use '_' for literal integers to improve readability.

245_000_000_000

The. Can now be used with the separator of decimals in order to create a 🚀 .

Number Types

There will be 2 numerical types within the Emojicode.

If 🔢 which will represent any number of integers within the interval $[-2^{63}+1, 2^{63}-1]$.

If 🚀 which is used as a store of the real number within an imitation that is common.

Symbol Literals

The symbol is the single Unicode character which represents the type of symbol 🈂️. If the type symbol is a representation of any character that is defined within Unicode, you can include the symbols within the code source file which is a prepending 🔟 prior to the symbol that is desired. This will be called the literal Symbol.

Example

percent 🔟%

Booleans

Emojicode has a type to represent Boolean values, which are true or false values. The type used to represent a Boolean value is 👋 and a truth value can be created by using 👍, while a false value can be created by using 👎. For example:

🍦 emojicodeIsTheFunniestLanguage 👍

🍦 phpIsAsCool 👎

Other Code Source Files to be Included

When an Emojicode is programmed it is compiled with a single file, always. Now, you can include the files of the other source code. This will insert the code that has been placed in the file at a point for which it is included.

Chapter Four

String 📜

The **String** is the value for another Emojicode file source meaning that the compiler is directed to the section of the code that includes the 📜 statement.

Comparing Strings

Using the equality method will help you determine if 2 strings represent the same value 😬.

😀 🍪🔤Straw🔤 🔤berries🔤🍪 🔤Strawberries🔤

The method call is used in the example above. 😬 represents a method that is defined in the 🔤 class. It is important to remember to call methods by placing an emoji before the method that must be called.

Concatenating Strings

To add two or more strings together (*concatenate*) you should use the 🍪 emoji. Wrap all strings you want to concatenate between two 🍪. The output will be one string.

🍦 string1 🔤Hello 🔤
🍦 string2 🔤my dear🔤

😀 🍪 string1 string2 🔤 World! 🔤 🍪

⊛scan be the most efficient way for strings that are concatenating so the compiler can ⊛ optimize the concatenation. Note that ⊛s are part of the language and are not simply just methods.

The syntax formally is:

String Pooling

At the time of compiling all the strings should be pooled to ensure that each literal string during runtime will be represented by that same object.

The first comparison will reference the objects and evaluate for true while the second won't evaluate for true.

😀 🔡Strawberries🔡 🔡Strawberries🔡 😀true
😀 😀🔡Straw🔡 🔡berries🔡😀 🔡Strawberries🔡 😀false

You should not use 😛 in order to compare strings. Use the 😁 instead.

String Mutability

Strings are immutable. You cannot modify any string. Instead, you can call methods within the strings which returns with a modified copy of the string that is original, then they themselves are considered immutable again.

Chapter Five
Lists

A mutable collection that is ordered and a set of values is called a list. They can be represented with the class. These sizes are unlimited theoretically and can be hardware that is practical. The fact that the Emojicode integers will have an upper bound will make them completely limited.

Lists are optimized fast by index access. You can access by append index, and pop with *O(1)*.

As in C or Java, the list that is being indexed will start at 0. The negative index can be assumed within a relative at the end of each list. This gives you an index of -1, which will be indicative of the very last index that is within this array, -2 will be the next to last of the elements within this array.

The Type

The class can be a generic that is needed for the type of value it can be. When using this class name, you must specify this argument that is generic. Next, you must specify the list that can hold those strings that you have written.

If the list you created is like this:

You should be able to add strings to the list that allow you to go right back to the string within the list. This syntax then gives the above list to Classes.

List Literals

You can create the list of the values which will denote the list between 🍹 and 🍆. You will have the ability to lower the list of values from the list that is between the 🍹 and the 🍆. This example is seen below.

14, 67, 2434

🐷 14 67 2434 🍆

Then the compiler tries to infer with a generic type of argument, s compiler will try to infer the generic type argument for the list.

list-literal → 🍹 [expressions] 🍆
expressions → expression | expression expressions

🍵 Dictionaries

Dictionaries are good for the use of assigning values to the key strings. Can be used to assign values to string keys. This dictionary is a theoretical one without limits.

Dictionary Literals

This shortcut is a syntax to create the dictionary.

dictionary-literal → 🍯 [kv-pairs] 🍆
kv-pairs → kv-pair kv-pairs | kv-pair
kv-pair → key expression
key → expression

The *key* absolutely has to be a string. This compiler has to try to infer the argument type that is generic for the dictionary. Below is an example of this within a dictionary for associate artists with birthplaces included.

⌗Aaron Copland⌗ ⌗Brooklyn⌗
⌗Michael Jackson⌗ ⌗Gary⌗
⌗Falco⌗ ⌗Vienna⌗

▶▶ Ranges

Emojicode range type called ▶▶ is supported. A range is an immutable sequence of numbers, as opposed to more strictly speaking integers. Ranges can be described by start, stop, and step. Every number contains:

⌗Aaron Copland⌗ ⌗Brooklyn⌗
⌗Michael Jackson⌗ ⌗Gary⌗
⌗Falco⌗ ⌗Vienna⌗

f(x) = star + x step and it matches the limits of start $\leq$ **f(x)** < stop within the element of each range. If the step becomes negative, the constraint stops < **f(x)** $\leq$ and begins to apply instead.

Ranges will be created when using the shortcut syntax, which depends on your needs.

range-literal ⟶ range-literal-with-step

This uses *1* as the *step* value since the *start* is lower than *stop*, otherwise -1 is used as the *step* value. If *0* is provided as *step* value, the *step* will become the set to an appropriate value as described before.

Ranges are very helpful when combined with  if you need to repeat anything for a specific number of times:

The end result from running the examples above will give you this below:

```
0
2
4
6
8
0
1
2
3
4
5
6
7
8
9
10
9
8
7
6
5
4
3
2
1
100
90
80
70
60
50
40
30
20
10
0
```

Chapter Six
Syntax

Due to the complexity of the language that is being described in this book you are going to need formal definitions from time to time. There will be some syntactic definitions within this language guide. If you do not have any concern for the definitions of syntax, then you have no worries. You will also be able to follow this without problems.

Notation

This guide uses a slightly modified grammar notation that is similar to BNF.

Hippo->rhinoceros

Panther->[*] hyena |*

Within the first line, there is an example of what we define by a rule of thumb as a *hippo*, which simply states a *hippo consists* of a *rhinoceros*. This is yet another rule which has been indicated by the background that is purple and the emoji that is .

The notation of grammar that we were using in this document follows the following rules:

- Every rule that begins with someone's name and -> (reads that it "consists within")

- The bar that is vertical (|) is used to separate all the alternatives.

- Example: *foo-> mouse dog (|) hippo*

- This will denote that the *foo* may consist of the *mouse* and the *dog*. It can also include only the *hippo*.

- Rules are able to be broken down into multiple starting lines that contain the same names. The line that is new is then the alternative that is within the content's right to use the -> which was then the same line within the previous definite but separated by a bar that is vertical.

- *Foo->mouse dog | hippo*

- As well as this one.

- *Foo->mouse dog*

- *Foo->hippo*

These will indicate the same exact thing.

- Parts can be enclosed in the bracket squares *([and])* which are optional: these can then occur; however, they do not have to.

- To improve formatting and never have terminals, use white spaces.

- The word **except** would indicate the terminals or non-terminals that should not appear, although the previous non-terminal which is indicative that it would appear. **except** may also appear multiple times one behind the other, the multiple values excluded.

Document Syntax

The Emojicode that is the source code for the document would consist of a number of document-statements.

document-statement->package-import | ![icon] | include | version

document-statement->[documentation-comment] type-definition

document-statement-> start-flag

include-> ![icon] string-literal

start-flag->![icon] return-type block

type-definition-> class | value-type| extension | protocol | enum

Expression and Statement

Statements are standalone elements within the Emojicode programming that portray the normal code of the program. These statements can either be large or small depending on the type of code you are writing.

statement->expression | frozen-declaration | assignment | declaration

statement-> superinitializer | return | error-check-control | error

statement-> if | for-in | repeat-while

frozen-declaration-> ![icon] variable expression

assignment->![icon] variable expression | ![icon] method-emoji variable arguments declaration->📝 variable type

expression->numerical-literal | 👍 | 👎 | symbol-literal | string-literal | 🐱

expression-> method-call | identity-check | nothingness | unwrap | is-nothingness

expression-> callable-call | method-capture | closure | type-method-call

expression-> list-literal | dictionary-literal | range-literal | concatenate-literal

expression-> supermethod-call | is-error | perfect-extraction | cast

expression-> metatype-instance | metatype-instance-from-instance | instantiation

symbol-literal-> 🔟 unicode

Variable and Emoji

unicode ⟶ any Unicode character defined in Unicode 9.0
emoji ⟶ see http://www.unicode.org/Public/emoji/4.0//emoji-data.txt
variable ⟶ variable-head [variable-parts]
variable-head ⟶ unicode except integer-prefix except number except emoji
variable-parts ⟶ variable-part | variable-part variable-parts
variable-part ⟶ unicode except emoji

Chapter Seven
Control Flow

Emojicode provides the user with different control flow statements that allow you the structure of the flow throughout the program.

Code Block 🍇 🍉

Code blocks can be used adjacent to the flow structure control which is a group statement which can be executed within the only condition that is met or not met and will be repeatable.

Syntactic Definition

clock-> 🍇 statements 🍉

statements-> statement statements | statement

Examples of these blocks which can be seen below.

🍉 if

The statement above says that 🍉 is a very important point. It allows the conditional execution within the block code. The whole syntax is:

If-> 🍉 condition block [else-ifs] [else]

Else-ifs-> else-if else ifs | else-if

Else-if -> 🍪 condition block

Condition-> expression | frozen-declaration

If the *condition* which evaluates the 👍 indicates the code block is being executed, and that it evaluates the 👎 which should be ignored.

The examples below will display that *a* is bigger than *b* and if *a* is bigger than *b*:

🍦 a 10

🍦 b 4

🍉▶ a b 🍇

😁 🔤 a is bigger than b 🔤

🍉

🍓

🍓 will extend to a 🍉 statement that is executed for an additional block within the case of the expression which is in the statement that has been evaluated to false. The next code would be to display a is greater than b if "a would be greater than b" and "a cannot be greater than b" which is stated below.

🍦 a 2

🍦 b 8

🍉▶ a b 🍇

😁 🔤 a is bigger b 🔤

🍉

^{AB}ca is not greater than b^{AB}c

This statement, is the only one executed if the statement which is evaluated for false, and then all the statements would be evaluated for false also.

will extend a statement which can be executed in a different statement in which the case can be described as the original condition, which is evaluated in the . Although, unlike the , it can execute the expressions that are alternative if only they were the which is . This makes the following code what would be displaying "*a* which is bigger as opposed to *b*," "*a* is equal with *b*" and "*a* which is smaller than the *b*."

a 2

b 7

 a b

^{AB}ca is bigger than b^{AB}c

 a b

😁 ᴬᴮcan equal to bᴬᴮc

😋

🍓 🍇

😁 ᴬᴮca is smaller than bᴬᴮc

😋

This 🍪 statement is executed once with the preceding 🍊 expressions and then with any preceding 🍪 expressions that are evaluated to 👎, as the current 🍪 is expressed and evaluated to 👍.

Reiterate with 🔁

This 🔁 will allow you to quickly iterate above the instance which is repeatedly trying to retrieve those values from the time that there are values and the time that there are no values left to be provided. You can iterate over the 🍨 instance and then you will receive the elements that are contained in this list. The 🔁 for the statement can iterate on top of the instances of any one of the types with which have been conformed to the 🔁🌀 within the Elemental protocol.

The syntax is:

for-in-> 🔁 *variable expression block*

Now the compiler will transform those statements into a bytecode that is equivalent to more statements that are rewritten to this code.

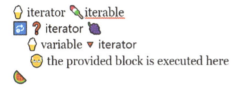

The *iterable* is an instance that will iterate on top and the *variable* in the name of the variable that is provided. As you can see, the variable can be a type that was provided for the argument that is generic within the *Element* when it is within the type of *iterable* that has been declared as its conformance to as an Element.

With this example, the block code will have repeated. All the values of that said list and the values *tree, bee, lee,* and *me* will eventually be printed. Then, the type of **name** can naturally be . This is due to facts that can be defined as Elements that can be declared in its conformance of and as **Element** which is, therefore, the return of an iterator for that type **Element** and this is what type the variable is inferred of. If in the event that you need to repeat something more often than once, then you must use **Ranges** within the combination with .

This Defines (Repeat While) 🔁

🔁 repeats the block code given under the circumstances that the condition uses 👍. This can mean that if the condition is not ever 👍, the block code shall never be executed. This syntax should say:

repeat-while-> 🔁 condition block

This example below means that for infinity it will print out the "disko disko partinzani."

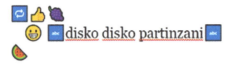

Since the ease of the use of the 🔀 statement 🔁 can only be used seldom.

Chapter Eight
The s Packages and Important Classes

Emojicode divides the code into packages. A package can be a unit within the code which can relate to more than one Emojicode file. These packages contain the name that is associated or defined similar to them, and every line of the code will then belong to that package. The compiler will identify this while executing the code, and the code written after the '_' will belong to that package. Remember that all the code that you will write belongs within that package.

Every package has its own namespaces and types. If you have imported or defined the types in one of the packages, the type should not be available in any other package that has been created without importing them explicitly into the package.

Importing Other Packages

The objective of each package is designed to provide you with an easy way to reuse the code. Naturally, you can simply import the other packages into this package that has been created. The syntax for doing this is listed below:

Package-import-> 🗂 *package-name emoji*
Package-name-> variable

When this statement is found in the code, the compiler begins to search for the Path for the Package Search within the package that is defined by the given name located at the package-name. This, then, will try to import into the program. This creates a default

Path for the Package Search which is local too /user/ local/ EmojicodePackages/ with the UNIX operating systems.

Once you import the package, you will see all types that have been exported within the imported package that will be made available for the imported package. Then, the types should be added to any of the given namespaces with the **destinationNamespace** in the event that this will cause the naming collision which works with the compiler to emit these errors. I will also note that the namespaces can be completely local to a specific package.

This brings us to the example below which imports these *files* into packages with the global namespace ●. Next, this program will be used for the class ▪ which was imported from the *files* package.

🗀 files ⬤
🏴🐌
💡 file ◆☐🗏 abc tests/fileTest_testFile.txt⬛
🔥

These packages will load the other packages, leading to a circular dependency. It will then detect these dependencies and work to abort those compilations.

This s package becomes imported implicitly within the namespace global of ● for every single package.

Making a Package Importable

The package is then placed in a single file which has a starting point of which is called, either **header.emojic** intended for the package that is importable or named arbitrarily for the _ package. This creates a file that is then able to include many other files by simply using 📜 .

All types become defined inside the package that is internal. They are also not exported. If you need to export the type, which is defined within your package, then you would be able to prepend it with 🌍 .

Extensions are then applied, always within the class extended, which can be explicitly marked with the 🌍 . Packages become cached in order to be available for extension, then they can only be applied to it once. When the packages extend, the class that has extensions can be available in all locations within the package. This is the extension it has been loaded into from somewhere else which is within the Emojicode program.

The types won't actually connect to the namespace. When you export the type within the namespace, it becomes completely irrelevant. All the exported types should be imported into those requested namespaces even though they are not within the namespace that they were exported into initially.

Another package that is importable also must declare that its version is using 🌙 :

```
version → [documentation-comment] 🌙 major minor
major → integer-literal
minor → integer-literal
```

That's when the **header.emojic** is of a simulated cat within the package that must look similar to this:

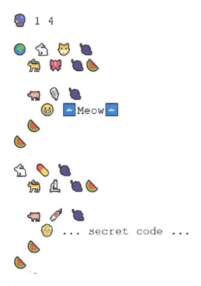

In order to create the package making it importable, finally, we can move those files to the Path of the Package Search. Each packages directory is individually named with **{name}-v{major}** and then the link that is symbolic will help to connect to their directory which could be named based on just that package.

So, the next step is to create a directory that has **cat-simulator-v1** and then the link **cat-simulator** is added to this directory. Then this directory should look similar to this:

```
            ...
         ├── s ->
/usr/local/EmojicodePackages/s-v1
         ├── s-v1
    |     └── header.emojic
         ├── cat-simulator ->
/usr/local/EmojicodePackages/cat-
         simulator-v0
         └── cat-simulator-v0
             └── header.emojic
```

If you were to import this package, you would receive access for the 🐱 however, you would not have access for the 💊 class since it is not exported-able.

Native Binaries

These packages should be accompanied with the compiled binary that is native. Native binaries will then be introduced with performance issues which are not so easy to maintain and they should only be used in situations when absolutely necessary.

In order to declare that the package will come with the native binary, you will place a 📻 within the document level.

After that you can use 📻 instead of the method and initializer bodies:

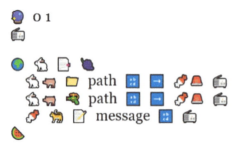

To implement the methods into the C, you should consult the manual that came with your virtual machines. Native APIs are not a standardized set and they aren't required for this type of language programming. The virtual machine is then able to reject the file for the bytecode so that it depends on the external binary that is native.

The Real-Time Engine for the Emojicode fully supports binaries that are native.

Package Register and Manager

The package registers along with the build a package manager is designed for easy install as well as updates and used packages that are planned to run.

Package Report

These can compile and then generate a JSON which is a report of the types of defined packages given. When generating the report comprised of all the files they are directly moved to the compiler using the *-r* option. Then, they will generate the reports for a specific package which should use *the* *-r packageName* option.

The s Packages

An s package is best compared to what's called a standard library in many of the other languages for programming. To write some of the most meaningful programs you can use this to provide you with those important classes and value types.

Example:

You have already been introduced to the types in previous sections within this book. The types listed above are defined within the s package.

Atomicity of the s Package

You should be really informed that none of the classes within the s package guarantee atomicity. When you access the s package structural data you need to always make sure that you use a mutex to avoid conditions of the race.

Chapter Nine
Classes, Enumerations and Value Types

Emojicode has three characteristics of object-orientation: *Value Types, Enumerations, and Classes.*

Concepts of Object-Orientation

There are four concepts associated with object-orientation.

Dynamic Lookup

Dynamic lookup is the object which it will have with the methods by which it is called dynamically executing its method. This allows the overriding and inheritance methods in the class.

Abstraction

Abstraction is the implementation of details that can be hidden in what is set as the public method in which you will provide a way that you can manipulate that stored data.

Subtyping

Subtyping states if this object has all the other objects functionality it is then a given that if an object has every bit of the functionality of a given type b can be used in the context of type b. Emojicode will accomplish this act using the protocols.

Inheritance

Inheritance allows you to reuse the definition of one type for another. However, it should be noted that only the classes will take advantage of all the concepts listed above, while each type of value as wells as enumerations can only provide an abstraction and/ or subtyping.

Difference between Classes vs Value Types.

There are major differences between classes and value types.

The instances of classes can always be allocated on top of the heap and are passed by the reference. Instances of value types can be as their name suggests and then passed by value.

Classes will feature inheritance while value types do not. Value Type methods are dispatched statically.

This makes the value types suitable for when the only actual data represented matters and not the identity of the object. In other words, you should only use value types in the instance that you only care about the values that they carry and not when you are concerned about if you have a specific instance of the value type.

Dates and the mathematical vectors can be good examples of the types that would be value types, whereas a type that is representing a customer needs to be a class, it matters with the specific customer instance that you're dealing with since all the instances represent one exact customer.

This is completely contrary to those examples for a date or a vector. You should not think of them as "the one you're working with." They must be abstract ideas and then only exist in our heads. You might write them down on a piece of paper, but then the piece of paper would become an instance of a class, which will store the data.

Defining a Class

This syntax is to define the class.

```
class → 🐭 type-identifier [generic-parameters] [superclass] type-body
type-body → 🐙 type-body-declarations 🍉
type-body-declarations → type-body-declaration | type-body-declaration type-body-declarations
type-body-declaration → type-body-attributes type-body-declaration-main
type-body-attributes → [documentation-comment] [ ⚠ ] [ 🔒 ] [access-level] [ ✏ ] [ 🐭 ] [ ✏ ] [ 🔍 ]
type-body-declaration-main → declaration | method | initializer
type-body-declaration-main → protocol-conformance | enum-value
superclass → type
```

If you happen to omit the *superclass,* then the class won't have a *superclass.*

For example, the code with which is laid out below will clearly define a class named 🐟, this contains no *superclass.*

We can now create a subclass that will exist for this 🐟 class and begin by declaring a 🐡 class that will represent a blowfish, which is a more concrete type of fish:

🐭 🐡 🐠 🍇

🍉

Classes are often used to represent a thing in the real world that you do not have to worry too much about. For example, you can write a class to define a customer since you must emphasize the customer you are dealing with and not only the data that the class holds. You may have many customers whose name is Jane Doe, but each customer is a different person and is therefore represented by a different object. Let us define a class that represents a customer.

✏️ 👤💼 🍇

🍉

To differentiate between the customers, we must add in some instance variables and an initializer.

✏️ 👤💼 🍇

    ✏️ 🆕 first_name 🔤

    ✏️ 🆕 last_name 🔤

    ✏️ 🆕 credit_card 💳

    🆕 ✏️ first_name 🔤 ✏️ last_name 🔤 ✏️ credit_card 💳
    🍇🍉

🍉

Variables

✏️ is used to declare a variable. You can declare a variable in two ways – you can declare the variable and assign it a value in one step or you can declare the variable and not give it a value initially.

5300 ➡️ ✏️ 🆕 money

✏️ 🆕 catName 🔤

The second variable is useless since there is no information stored in that variable. This situation can be changed easily by including instance variables. An instance variable cannot be accessed from another program or method.

In the program above, we have included a variable that provides some information about the credit card. If you want to include more information about the card, you can include instance variables for that credit card.

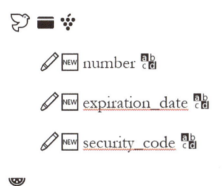

Remember that the most important aspect of Emojicode will be that they work to enforce initialization with all variable instances.

Defining a Value Type

This syntax will define a value type that is listed below.

value-type → 🐱 type-identifier [generic-parameters] type-body

Hint

These specific types are well-defined types which are immediately available in the namespaces that are provided.

Initializers

Initializers are responsible for preparing the instance for which you use and can be called to instantiate the type that is going to gain the instance of the given type.

The syntax which is able to define the initializer is shown below:

initializer → 🐖 [init-error] name [init-parameters] block
init-parameters → init-parameter | init-parameter init-parameters
init-parameter → [🔴] variable type
init-error → 🔺 type

In the initializer, all the instance variables are those which must be initialized.

If you are then initializing a class for an instance which has a class that includes a superclass, you must call an initializer of the superclass. The 🐖 is the keyword that is used to call a *super initializer*.

superinitializer → 🐖 superinitializer [arguments]

By then enforcing the rules, Emojicode can then guarantee that all instance of this type is always going to be fully initialized when it is obtained from the initializer.

You can see this in the following example of the initializer for the 🐟 class:

🐖 🏔 ageGiven 🔤 nameGiven 🐿 🔢 🐙
  🍦 age ageGiven
  🍦 name nameGiven
  🍦 speedInM/s o
🍉

This initializer will initialize all the variables to the appropriate values. **Age** and **name** are initialized to the values that are passed by arguments. **speedInM/s** was also set to a few default values.

Initializers are value types that work quite similarly, with one of the big differences being in contrast to the class initializers that they return of the value. This will change in a further version of Emojicode.

Variables from Arguments can be Initializing Instances

Because this is so common that the instance of variables is initialized from the arguments, there's a shortcut that heads straight to this 🔒. 🔒 can be used in front of those variable names that are of the argument and then they automatically copy the value of which is passed into the instance that is the variable with the same name.

The example above improved with 🔒:

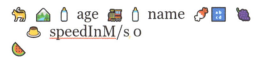

Instantiation

To get the instance of value type or a class, you must instantiate it. ◆ can be used for instantiation.

The syntax is:

instantiation → ◇ type-expr initializer [arguments]

The *initializer* should be the name for the initializer that you want to use. Naturally, you should have a correct number of arguments that are appropriate and the correct number.

To get the  for the instance and example is listed below:

◆🐟🏠 2 🔤Billy🔤

Enumerations

Enumerations are special types of programming with values that represent a specific set of options from several to choose from which one can be chosen.

Defining an Enumeration

The syntax that is needed to define the enumeration is:

enum → 🐖 type-identifier type-body
enum-value → 🔘 emoji

This will work for a simple example:

With this example, the enumeration can be named 🍴 and it is defined by what offers the values 🍠, 🍤 and 🍔.

Instantiating an Enumeration

With each enumeration that is automatically able to provide the initializers for whatever options, the name that is after the option should be the instance which will be represented. This, like any other value type, is the instantiated or enumerated one with :

Enumerations are not able to have custom initializers.

Chapter Ten
Methods

Methods are blocks of code that are bound to the type: a class or value type.

The syntax used to define a method is given below.

method ⟶ 🐖 method-emoji [generic-parameters] [parameters] [return-type] block
parameters ⟶ parameter | parameter parameters
parameter ⟶ variable type
return-type ⟶ ➡️ type

Another example for the 🐟 class:

```
🌮 Swim the given distance within one hour. 🌮
🐖 🏊 distanceInMeters 🚀 🍇
  🍮 speedInM/s ➗ distanceInMeters 3600
🍉
```

Every method returns some value. By looking in the syntax definition, you can declare the return types. If there is no return type and it was declared as the return type, then it defaults to ✨. 🍎 and is used to explicitly for the return of a value:

return ⟶ 🍎 expression

Here is another great example from the 🐟 class that is using 🍎:

```
🌮 Determines whether this fish should retire. 🌮
🐖 👴 ➡️ 👌 🍇
  🍎 ▶️ age 4
🍉
```

This type of method can return true when the fish is much older than four years. Let us also define the method for the 📅 value type:

🍞 Whether the year of the date is a leap year. 🍞
🐖 🍁 🔙 💧 🍢
🍎 🌰 😫📱 year 4 0 🐢 ▶️📱 year 100 0 😫📱 year 400 0
🍉

There is a list of reserved emojis with which cannot be used in the method names. These can be found at the end.

Calling Methods

The following syntax can be used to call a method:

method-call → method-emoji callee [generic-arguments] [arguments]
callee → expression
arguments → expression | expression arguments

Method-emoji is the method's name with which you call. **Callee** is an instance with which the method should be called. Of course, all the arguments must be provided as they are required.

Now look at this example of the 🐟 class:

💡 michaelTheFish 🔷🎁🏠 3 🔤Michael🔤
🏠 michaelTheFish 300

🍞 😀 michaelTheFish 🐋
  😫 🔤Michael will retire!🔤
🍉

Every emoji with which you do not find a language defined or an expression, you will find that it is a method call.

You will often need to get the instance with which the method was called, this is the value or the object. This is what 🐌 is for.

🐑 returns that the current value, whose initializer or method was being called.

In this example, the 🐟 calls another method which determines if the fish from the first method should retire or if it can sign a new contract for employment:

```
🌮 Signs a new contract of employment. 🌮
🐖 🖊 🐈
🍊 😊 🐕 🐈
     😄 abc Sorry, I'd prefer to retire. abc
🍉
     🍅 🐈
     😄 abc I hope they'll pay me twice as much. abc
🍉
🍉
```

Note that with the initializer, you won't be able to use 🐑 before the object is fully initialized. This happens before all the instance variables are set, and then the superinitializer gets labeled. Since this is allowed, you can call the methods for using the instance. Then you might access the instance variable which has not been initialized yet.

Type Methods

You can define the type methods which will be called on the type and not on the instance of the type.

The type methods are then defined as a normal method however with the 🖊 attribute. The example below will explain:

 Returns the available pizzas.

Since the type methods don't completely execute in the object context, they use the 🐕 which is illegal. The type methods are also then inherited by the subclasses.

Calling Type Methods

You can use the following syntax to call the type method:

type-method-call → 🍩 method-emoji type-expr [generic-arguments] [arguments]

Examples include:

🍩 🧱 🍕

This will then allow you to call the type method 🧱 on the class 🍕, and we define this above.

Reserved Emojis

However, the emojis cannot be part of the method names.

method-emoji → emoji except reserved-emoji
reserved-emoji → 🍩 | 🍩 | 🏠 | 🌀 | 🌀 | 💡 | 🥤 | 🔍 | 🍪 | 🔎
reserved-emoji → 🥟 | 🥡 | 🔁 | 🔂 | 🍊 | 🍩 | 🍆 | 🍪 | 🍓 | 🥒
reserved-emoji → 🦴 | 🍎 | ⬜ | ⬛ | ⬜ | ◆ | 🐕 | ⚡ | ⬭ | 🍪
reserved-emoji → 🔡 | 😀 | 🔟 | 👍 | 👎 | 😀

Assignments by Call

Assignment by Call is a method that can quickly replace the content of your variable with some results of the method that is called on within its value.

 counter 1

 counter 1

At the end of the code snippet, the value of the counter will be 2.

The 2nd line will work exactly like  counter ➕ counter 1.

```
 counter 1
➕ counter 1
```

Any of these methods will be utilized in any assignment that is called just to make sure that it returns those types of variables. This method could take any number of some arguments, which in the following print for the value friends is utilized in any Assignment by Call. Just make sure that it returns the type of the variable.

```
 counter 1
➕ counter 1
```

Access Levels

These access levels can be described within the context of a method or initializer which can be called. There can be 3 access levels.

access-level ⟶ 🔒 | 🔒 | 🔓

🔓: This can be accessed from anywhere for the method or initializer.

🔒: This can be defined as any type of method or initializer which can be accessed within any type.

🔒❓: This can be accessed by the clashes, weapons, and many others. This method is used to access within the type class allowing the class that inherits the class that can be defined by the method.

Deprecation

The methods of initializers are needed to be deprecated. Emojicode allows for the mark of a method that is deprecated with an ⚠ attribution.

The computer is then emitting a warning for whenever the deprecated method is used.

Identity Check

😛 this can be used for determining the two objects that are in reference to the points with which the same object is in memory.

This is not an equality check. The two objects represent what might be the same value, but they have two different objects which are still not able to share the same location of memory. To determine the equality, we use 😀 if available.

identity-check → 😀 expression expression

returns the truth of the results that both expressions have in reference to some of the same locations for memory. The expression's result must be compatible with the ●.

Protocols

This protocol is defined by the methods for which a functionality that is special. The protocols can only describe the methods a class is necessary to have to support this functionality. Next, the classes must conform to the protocols and you must work on implementing all the methods and declaring the conformation.

Defining the protocol will help define the type. All the classes should agree to that protocol and are compatible with this story type.

Declaration

These definitions of syntax are good for the protocol which is similar to the way that you are defining a class:

protocol → 🐍 type-identifier protocol-body
protocol-body → protocol-method | protocol-method protocol-body
protocol-method → [documentation-comment] [⚠] 🐷 method-emoji arguments return-type

For example:

Here we have declared this protocol that is named ◎. With all the classes that will be conformed within this protocol, you will have to implement more of the methods ♫. This doesn't give us all the protocol but tells us that any one of the actual types can conform to

⊙ and they are capable of playing some music, however, they must initialize 🎶 method.

Using the normal 🐄 to help you get the required instance of methods which is inside the 🦫 body. This is at present the only one that is possible within its own possible initializers process or methods type.

Chapter Eleven
Optional

✦ Nothingness

The nothingness is a value that is used when you need to represent the missing value. The methods are many that return nothingness on failure. The method that does not declare explicitly can return types that are assumed to have a nothing returns.

To get Nothingness you use:

nothingness ⟶ ⚡

Since the nothingness can be a completely valid type and the value is often its own, then it's used normally in the conjunction with the optional.

Optional 🍬

The optional can be a way to ensure the type is optional. This is like saying that something is either not declared a type or its ⚡. The optional can be very useful within the cases of where the value

seems to be missing for the method that might fail and 🍎 then nothing takes place instead of the expected value.

To make the type optional, you must prepend it as a 🍬.

Examples:

🔘 first 🐌 🔡Kumquat🔡 0
🔘 twelfth 🐌 🔡Kumquat🔡 11

Many methods return ⚡ when they fail. The method 🐌 with which 🔤 and the method returns the 🔢 within the given index for ⚡.

🔘 first 🐌 🔡Kumquat🔡 0
🔘 twelfth 🐌 🔡Kumquat🔡 11

You can identify **first** and then you will contain a will 🔢 and **twelfth** will only contain ⚡.

You will then have the optional point which provides you with more safety. This can be achieved with the forcing of the programmer to take special care with the optional and the optional should not be used in a similar way to the type they made optional.

Unwrapping 🍺

If you want the value to be **first** or **twelfth** from within the example above, you can unwrap the optional using 🍺:

unwrap → 💀 expression

This will tell the Emojicode to check what value there is that is not ⚡ and then returns it. If the value is ⚡, then the program should be terminating within the error message as shown below:

🚨 Fatal Error: Unexpectedly found ✨ while unwrapping a 🍬.

Naturally, you are unwrapping the optional that is without the check which is not safe and should not be done. See these sections in the example below for safe ways.

Nothingness Test

If you can use ☁ in order to test with an optional which is ⚡.

is-nothingness → ☁ expression

☁ can return 👆 and the expression will be ⚡.

Condition Assignment 🍈🍦

There is a more useful way to protect the value of ⚡ which is connected to the assignment conditions. You are able to use 🍦 within the conditions. These have some combinations that which is in common with the 🍈, 🍪, or 🔁, and the condition will be 👆 if the value provided for the variable is not ✨. Within this case, you will see the variables that will set all the unwrapped value.

This example below will help you understand:

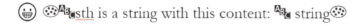

🍉

Then, the block of that 🍊 statement can be executed within the ⬛ sth, 🔤 does not need the evaluate to ✨.

Chapter Twelve
Extensions

The extensions will allow you to soon extend those that you have to an existing value type or class. In the extension, you will declare and then define every single thing that you can do when you initially are declaring a class or value type. This will include methods, type methods, and protocol conformity.

Cution

Add some instance variables and the depreciation which is 0.5.4 and this will be a removal of the upcoming version of the Emojicode.

The syntax is defined below:

extension → 🐋 type-identifier type-body

You should also be able to extend the classes within the other packages. This example is simple:

Circumvent Dependencies that are Circular

An extension which can also be used within the program to circumvent any circular dependencies that arise. Imagine this problem:

It doesn't matter the order in which the class is defined, this example is a compilation. This is the problem that can be solved easily using extensions.

Even though the extensions to the class are cost-free or thereabouts, it is considered good style to always be declaring forward with classes that will extend later.

Chapter Thirteen
Inheritance and Overriding

Inheritance allows for instances of a more concrete type to share their attributes with subclasses. When you use a subclass for the class, the subclass will inherit some or all methods and method types. Initializers are then the only inherited class under those conditions that are special.

Initializer Inheritance

In the Emojicode, the initializers can all be inherited by the subclasses but only if the subclass meets the following criteria:

- It cannot define any instance of variables within the subclass.

- It cannot define any initializer within the subclass.

- It cannot fulfill all these criteria within the subclass. It also is not allowed for the subclass to inherit any initializers.

Required Initializers

All subclasses in the class must have an initializer. With this, the required initializer needs to be used. Once the initializer is marked, it is required to have the 🍬 attribute. Subclasses shall implement all the initializers that have been marked with 🍬 attribute even if they cannot be eligible for the initializer and inheritance. These initializers can again be marked with 🍬, and thereby they are enforcing that all the descendants within the original class be provided with the required initializer.

This simple example will define what an initializer 🌱 will do for all descendants of 🌼 and what it must provide:

```
🐇 🏠 🐚
  🔍 🐖 🌱 🐚 🔵 Every flow can be constructed by seeding it
  🐚

🐇 🐖 🏠 🐚
  🔵 The sunflower just inherits the initializers
  🐚

🐇 🌺 🏠 🐚
  🔵 The hibiscus additionally stores its color
  🍠 color 🔢
  🔵 Therefore, we must implement 🌱 ourselves and set color to some default
  🔍 🐖 🌱 🐚
    🍠 color 🔶red🔶
    🐿 🌱
    🐚
  🔵 An initializer to get an hibiscus with a specific color
  🐷 🔵 🐚 color 🔢 🐚
    🐿 🌱
    🐚
  🐚
```

Overriding Methods

The subclass is something that can be overridden with a method that is defined in a superclass. That is the way they provide a new implementation of it.

The method has been overridden by being redeclared with it in the subclass that contains the 🔲 attribute. This simple example will assist you:

```
🐇 🌼 🐚
  🐷 🕐 time 🇫🇷 🐚
    🔵 Open and close the blossom according to the time...
    🍉
  🍉

🐇 🌼 🐖 🐚
  🖊 🐷 🕐 time 🇫🇷 🐚
    🔵 Sunflowers also rotate to face the sun....
    🐬 🕐 time 🔵 Open and close like other flowers; see below
    🍉
  🍉
```

Calling Super Methods

Inside a method you can use this syntax to call the super method:

supermethod-call ⟶ 🐿 method-emoji [arguments]

This we simply will call the super method named method-emoji and it returns the value. You have already seen an example that can explain this process.

Promises

You must be conscious and watch out to not break the superclass's promises which have been designated for when to override these methods. It promises that there are a few sets of rules that will ensure that the required initializers and methods are of the same class and are being used in the way that they should be for the ones that have a superclass. The main characters of any object can be found through orientation. These promises are listed below:

- The initializer or method within the subclass must take the same amount of arguments.

- The return type can be any form of initializer or method within this subclass that must be the same or a similar subtype. The subtype is the return of the subclass which must be the same or a subtype of the return type of the overridden initializer or method.

- The arguments of this initializer or method for this subclass will be of the same type as well as a supertype for the argument types within the overridden or initialized methods.

- The initializer or method of the subclass should have the exact same access for the modified that has the superclass with the super method and initializer must have the same access modifier as the super method or initializer.

Error Handling

There are proper mechanisms which can handle the errors which are an integral part of what is modern language in programming. Being that Emojicode is a modern language, Emojicode can provide an advanced, sophisticated, however light-weight way to maintain and handle errors.

Chapter Fourteen
The 🚨 Types

The Emojicode can provide a unique type of way that allows you the ability to handle error codes. These unique ways are called 🚨 types. A 🚨 type can always be composed of two types of services: An enumeration which serves as an *error enumeration* will indicate all the kinds of errors which occur within a contained type. This type can be presented if there are absolutely no errors that arise.

A great example of this is the method that would normally be the return of 🔤 which can then be declared that it will have a returned instance of 👥, in this case of this specific error you get this:

🐷 😋 → 🚨 👥 🔤 🍇

Another instance of this 🚨 type is going to either contain the error in that form of enumerations and value or a separate contained type of value.

The 🚨 Statement

This is an error with which you can find in the instance that it was created and then raised within the function. With this specific function, the 🚨 statement works to be like 🍎. This can also be used to create the error that returns a function. Consider this syntax.

error → 🚨 expression

With this expression, you must evaluate within the instance of the error that is enumerated. This example listed below will show a class, within this class stands the Emojicode for a microphone. There is a method that is called  which might fail in more than one case where an error is returned.

Error Initializer

Since the initializers can fail as well, Emojicode will also allow you to initialize the return errors. The error will have an enumeration which is declared right after the 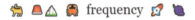 like this:

In a contained value they must not be provided since the contained value is obviously the specific type that is instantiated.

Here's the example of the initializer which returns an error:

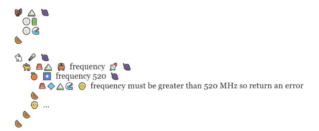

Control Error Check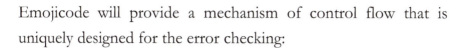

Emojicode will provide a mechanism of control flow that is uniquely designed for the error checking:

error-check-control →  variable expression block 🎛 variable block

The 🐚 can work in a sort of straightforward way. If your expression is evaluated to be an 🔲 instance, then it does not have to represent an error. The very first block will be executed as a variable that is set to a unique value which can be contained in the 🔲. If they indicate 🔲 and it does represent that there is an error, then the 🍓 within the block can be entered in its variable which is set to run the correct error enumeration within the instance.

Example:

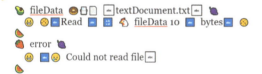

Test for Errors ⌐⌐⌐

Test whether the error 🔲 is an instance that represents a unique error, or the ⌐⌐⌐ is an expression which is just being used.

The syntax can be expressed below:

is-error → ⊙⊙⊙ expression

⌐⌐⌐ returns 👍 if the value is about an error or 👎 a false if it has not been an error and doesn't contain a value.

Perfect Extraction 🎦

If you are sure that this 🚨 instance will never create a representation of an error that you can use within the 🎦 expression which takes the contained value without having the prior error check.

The syntax can be represented as:

perfect-extraction → 🚊 <u>expression</u>

If the 🚨 is the instance which represents the error at the runtime, then the program will possibly abort with some sort of run-time error like:

🔺 Fatal Error: Unexpectedly found 🔺 with value 2.

Compatibility of the 🚨 Type

🚨 types can be intentionally shown as not compatible to the other types which are designed to enforce a prompt error handling. 🚨 types are the only compatible ones to the other types which have the exact same error that has been enumerated and contains a new type that is contained.

Chapter Fifteen

Documentation

Documentation is one of the most important parts of writing good code. Therefore, Emojicode can offer the built-in tools to document your source code.

Documentation Comments

Emojicode has the support for a special type of comments with which can be called *Documentation Comments*. The syntax can be used in one of these documentation tokens listed below:

documentation-comment → 🍩 documentation-comment-characters 🍩
documentation-comment-characters → documentation-comment-character | documentation-comment-characters
documentation-comment-character → except 🍩

Documentation allows comments so that it can only occur at locations that are specific:

Before an enum, class, value type, or protocol declaration:

🍩
   A class whose instances shall be enumerable using the 🔂 loop must
implement this protocol.
🍩
🔵 🐋 🔂🐀Element⭕ 🐌

🍋

Before you use a method, type the initializer declaration or method:

🍩
   This method must return an instance of a class that conforms to
<a href="1f361.html">🔍 </a> which will be used to enumerate this instance.
🍩
🐷 🔍 🔠 🔍🐀Element

81

The packages are before the so you can add the documentation about the whole package:

🫔
 The sockets package allows you to open TCP sockets to servers or to create a TCP server socket
 yourself.

 The following is a very basic example...
🫔
🧑 0 1

The comments are traditionally using Markdown. All these packages which ship with the Emojicode can be documented in this way and they are automatically compiled within the Package Index within this documentation. The compiler for this documentation will also support the additional syntax that is about auto-linking types, which is `<a href="74.html">type-emoji</a>` and can automatically be linked to the exact type within the package.

Reporting

Are the documentation comments inside the compiler helping to make you aware of what it is not just as a comment but the documentation for a specific method package, or type?

You can take advantage of this and have to tell the compiler to help with generating the report of a specific package that is using the **-r**, which can report on the package **-R packageName**, and the **_**, with which it will report on the package and whose name was provided. The compiler can only be a report on the packages that were already loaded within this program.

The example below is about how to run **Emojicode -Ra sockets server.**emojic to produce something that is similar to an abridged and formatted form:

```
{
  "documentation": "\n   The sockets package allows you to...",
  "valueTypes": [],
  "classes": [
    {
      "name": "🔌",
      "genericArguments": [],
      "documentation": "\n 🔌 represents a socket that listens ...",
      "methods": [
        {
          "name": "📞",
          "access": "🔒",
          "returnType": { "package": "sockets", "name": "📞", "optional":
true },
          "genericArguments": [],
          "documentation":"\n    Waits until a client wants to ...",
          "arguments": []
        }
      ],
      "initializers":[
        {
          "name": "🔲",
          "access": "🔒",
          "canReturnNothingness": true,
          "genericArguments": [],
          "documentation": "\n    Creates a 🔌 instance that immediately
...",
          "arguments": [
            {
              "type":{ "package": "s", "name": "🔢", "optional": false },
              "name": "port"
            }
          ]
        }
      ],
      "classMethods": [],
      "conformsTo": []
    }
  ],
  "enums": [],
  "protocols": []
}
```

The compiler can also display the documentation in the error message when you considered an appropriate method of deprecated.

Chapter Sixteen
Generics

Although Emojicode 0.5 has already released the documentation, it is not updated enough to show all the changes and modifications. The *Generics* will allow you to write some of the code in which you can use a placeholder such as variable names, instead of the actual name type, which can then be substituted with a real type that is available when you use the source code later. This can be a really powerful feature and is a wonderful way to be able to avoid duplication of the code.

Defining a Generic Class

To define the Generic class, you must define a class first and then append this code for each of the generic arguments that the class shall take:

```
generic-parameter → 🄶 variable type
generic-parameters → generic-parameter generic-parameters | generic-parameter
```

This structure can be called a *generic argument*. The *variable* is then named for the argument. The *type* is used as a generic argument constraint and these types tend to provide for this argument with what must be a compatibility with the constraints.

In this class body, you can reference the generic type of arguments that are labeled by name.

See this example for the "box" which can store the objects.

Sub-Classing a Generic Class

You can naturally subclass a specific generic class. You will have to provide values for the specific superclasses for the generic arguments. This can look like this example below:

🖊 ☑ 🎁 🐚 🔤 💐

🍉

If the subclass is taken as a generic argument, then this argument will be used within the argument of the superclass:

🖊 ✴ 🐚 A ⬤ 🎁 🐚 A 💐

🍉

Compatibility

Generic classes with the arguments can only be compatible if they have the same exact argument. So 🍼🐚🔤 can only be compatible with this class 🍼🐚🔤, but not with this class 🍼🐚⚪ even though you would expect it to be.

This following example cannot be compiled and then illustrated for why this kind of type is a conversion which is not allowed.

💡 listOfStrings 🍥 🔼Curiosity🔽 🔼Doesn't🔽 🏷️

📬 listOfSomethings 🍥🍛○
🍥 listOfSomethings listOfStrings
😕 Our list of strings is now suddenly a list of somethings
😕 (remember listOfSomethings points to the same list as listOfStrings)

👾 listOfSomethings 13 😕 Add an integer

📋 string listOfStrings 🏷️
  😵 The program would crash as there's an integer in our list of strings
  😋 string
🍐

Generic Methods and Initializers

It's also possible to define a generic method, type method, or initializer in a type that takes generic arguments within them and can be used as the argument types, and then return the type or as a type within the body.

A good example from this standard library is 🍺's 🐰 method. It is defined like this:

🐀 🐰 🔘AO callback 💐Element→A🐂 → 🍺🔘A 💐

😎 ...

🍉

The above code has one generic parameter which is named A and it is restricted to subtypes of ○, that can be of any type. You can call this method to know that you have provided the generic type arguments after those objects or classes are the ones which you call the method:

🍨 list 🍺🅰️🅱️caa🅰️🅱️c 🅰️🅱️c12345🅰️🅱️c 🍾

🐰 list 🔘🅰️🅱️cd 💐 a 🅰️🅱️cd → 🅰️🅱️cd

🍎 😵a 🅰️🅱️cds

🍉

87

The grammar for generic arguments can be:

generic-arguments → generic-argument | generic-argument generic-arguments
generic-argument → ⓖ variable type

However, in Emojicode you are capable of automatically inferring those arguments that are generic on your own by simply just writing:

🐰 list 🍇 a 🆎 ➡️ 🆎

🍎 🎨a 🅰🅱️c!

🍉

The Emojicode can automatically provide 🆎 as a representation of the argument that is generic for A.

Generic Protocols

You can define the generic protocols. Generic protocols will work in very similar or generic classes and have the same compatibility rules which apply.

A generic protocol is what you might use for 🔁.

🐌 🔁🔘Element🅾 🍇

🐷 🔩 ➡️ 🔩🔘Element

🍉

This takes one argument that is generic **Element** and determines the argument that is generic for the iterator (🔩) the 🔩 method must be returned.

The class that is conforming to this specific protocol must also pass the generic argument, like the class string below for the example:

 ...

 ...

 ...

Chapter Seventeen

Callable

The Emojicode supports blocks of codes called callables that can be compared to functions in other programming languages. Callables are like objects, but they can be stored within variables, and passed as an argument, etc.

Type

The callable type is declared as being used as the syntax:

callable-type → 🍇 [type-list] [return-type] 🍉
type-list → type | type type-list

Each *type* will stand for the argument of this type. You can then specify the *returnType*. If there is no return type that is specified, then the callable is assumed to return the value of Nothingness.

Examples:

🍇📘➡️🔢🍉 😀Takes an integer argument and returns a string
🍇➡️🔣🍉 😀Takes no arguments and returns a symbol
🍇🍉 😀Takes no arguments and returns nothing(ness).

Calling a Callable

The 🍭 must be used to call a callable.

callable-call → 🔍 expression [arguments] *This expression* should be a callable. You must also provide them with the required amount of correctly typed parameters to exist.

Example of calling a callable:

💀 greet is of type 🍇🔤🔤➡️

🍭 greet 🔤Bob🔤

Closure

Closures are blocks full of code that are immediately executable, but they maintain the context in which they were created. The variables and the method context can be passed around the program. The type of a closure is, of course, a callable.

A closure can then be created by the block of code which appears when the expected expression is available. This means that all the code blocks can be a part of an 🍓, 🍊, 🍋, 🔁, or 🔂 statement for the initializer or method of a declaration, which is a closure.

In contrast to the normal code block, the closure can be defined by arguments and then return a type that is similar to the method.

Formally, it's a syntax that is used in this way:

closure → 🍇 [arguments] [return-type] statements 🥭

The example is listed below:

🍦 greet 🍇 name 🔤 ➡️ 🔤

🏐 out 🔤🔤

🔂 i ⏩ ➖ 🐤 name 1 -1 🍇

🏐 out 👄 out 🥛 😀 name i

🍉

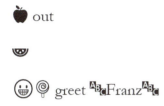

The above code is a very simple example of the closure which simply will reverse the given string along with the output:

Let's look at a more advanced use of a closure:

Here you can see the type method which returns the closure. This closure will close over the **name** variable which is here and then copies the value so that it will be used with the closure when it is called later.

Metatypes

Emojicode will allow you to pass a specific amount of certain types of values that can be called when the method type is instantiated.

Metatypes are types that are values or classes. The metatype of this type is the normal type prefixed name by ⬜:

metattype → ⬛ type

The metatype that is 🔠 can also be ⚪🔠 and then the metatype would be 🚂 equaling ⚪🚂. A variable which holds this type of metatype 🐟 class can look like this:

🍰 fishType ⚪🐟

To get the instance for such metatypes, in other words, the type that has value can be used with the ⬛ statement:

metatype-instance ⟶ ⬛ type

This *type* must be an identifying type identifier and the type whose metatype will be available. This metatype is then treated like other values.

The only metatypes that are available are the classes.

To populate those variables, you must pull from the above example and this code should be used:

🔔 fishType ⚪🐟

☐ can now be used to get the type of the type instance which is needed. The bottom syntax is a great example:

metatype-instance-from-instance ⟶ ☐ expression

This is used in order to instantiate another instance that is similar in type with which the method can be called:

🐗 🦄 ❀

♦⬛☐🐈ᴺᴱᵂ

👁

The following example of metatypes is listed in the stores of three different instances for the metatype in the list. This will instantiate them at the run-time and then calls a method for these instances:

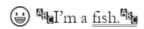

 I'm a fish.

 I'm a blowfish.

 I'm a whale.

🍉

🍉

✏️ 🐡 🐟 🍇

🔤 🔑 🐕 NEW 🍇 🐕 NEW 🍉

🔤 🐖 👶 🍇

😁 🔤I'm a tropical fish.🔤

🍉

🍉

🏁 🍇

🍨 classes 🍧⬜🐟 ⬜🐠 ⬜🐙 ⬜🐡 🍐

🔁 class classes 🍇

🍨 fish ◆⬛ class NEW

👶 fish

🍉

🍉

Chapter Eighteen
Memory Management

All the objects that are created will be placed on the heap. The heap will hold a memory for that area which is allocated when the Real-Time Engine will start up. When the heap becomes full when a garbage collection is performed, this can then automatically clean up the heap by removing inaccessible objects.

Garbage Collection

Emojicode will automatically manage those heaps and then dispose of the objects which then cannot be accessed anymore. The object is then considered to be inaccessible when there are absolutely no references to it. Since then the Engine in Real-Time will use a Garbage Collector, and then the references that are circular can be dealt with and it does not cause the objects to persist.

Clashing with the Garbage Collector

An important thing when creating the package binary is that you should take the Garbage Collector off. We may all have a love for the Garbage Collector, but it can become your enemy when you are trying to create a binary package.

Invocation of the Garbage Collector

To invoke the Garbage Collector within the Emojicode when you are performing these actions is done by calling the Garbage Collector Invoking Action, or GCIA.

1. Memory allocation

2. Calling a method or callable

3. Another function which performs any set of actions above, and refers to the documentation of the files in the header

Within the Garbage Collector sector, the function is to invalidate the objects which it cannot locate a reference for. It is not able to detect the reference to an object which you have in C++ style variables. Store all your references to objects within a safe place prior to performing the GCIA. This should help you achieve by use of retaining.

Garbage Collection and Threading

When in an environment of a multi-threaded Emojicode, the Garbage Collector requires some further care. It can only run fluently while all threads are paused, this would be the "stop the world" function. This may not stop the code or affect you, however, you can actually consider this when you have implemented the time-consuming actions. When utilizing Real-Talk Engine, your role is to ensure that the procedure doesn't limit the Garbage Collectors functions, unlike Emojicode, you cannot have control of the code. If the procedure is taking an extra long-time then you may want to consider trying:

```
void allowGC () ;
voiddisallowGCSndPauseIfNeeded () ;
```

When you call out *allowGC* you can allow the Garbage Collector to process at all times while the other tedious work is going on. Once the handler is completely done with the work, you must call *disallowGCAndPauseIfNeeded.*

Between the call of action *allowGC* and disallowGCAndPauseIfNeeded you should participate in the allocations for other types of GCIA, this will prevent you and the other functions that cannot have a call of action *allowGC*. The Garbage Collector tends to move any number of objects. Make sure that you are not relying heavily on any one of these, especially those that are retained, and not the objects within those two call functions. In order to complete the function, you need to understand that *void pauseForGC();* is an option but is not recommended since it is the function that is called within the execution of individual Emojicode instructions, which determines if the Garbage Collector has requested for that thread to pause.

Memory Management for the Engine in Real-Time

Memory management is performed at the same time across all points, except for when there is no space left in the memory. At such instances, garbage collection takes place.

Chapter Nineteen
Creating Your First Program

Compile and Run Your First Program

The Basic Structure

All Emojicode source files should bear the extension '.emojic.' Start by creating a file called **greeter.emojic** and put some content into it:

🏁 🍇

🍉

This becomes the minimum structure that every program must include. 🏁 becomes the special part within the language after which comes the code block. Every code block will begin with 🍇 and ends with 🍉 .

When the program is run, the code block after 🏁 is executed.

Greetings

We must add a greeting.

🏁 🍇

😀 🔤Howdy, partner!

🍉

Now let's try it out.

Hint

Open your command-line and then navigate to the directory that contains **greeter.emojic**. Then run this command.

Emojicode greeter.emojic

This then asks the compiler to compile greeter.emojic. When it goes well you should just simply exit without a message and then generate a file called greeter.emojib. This is your Emojicode Byte-Code File and this can be executed by the Engine Emojicode Real-Time.

Now type:

Emojicode greeter.emojib

Way to go! You've now written your very first program.

But does it work properly?

It's simple: 🔤Howdy, partner! Is a string literal.

Warming Up

Let's call a few more methods to warm up. We'll now write a method to convert English into *Pig Latin*. This is a very easy language simply because in order to get the Pig Latin word you will just need to move the very first letter of the word in English to the very end of the word and then add *ay*.

In Emojicode, you can easily extend all your existing classes, so we'll extend your string class to be able to convert words in English to Pig Latin. Place this into the following file:

🐷 🔤 🍇 tells it to Extend the class 🔤 (That's the string class).

🐖 🐮 ➡ 🔤 declares a new method called 🐮 and causes a return of an instance of the 🔤 class.

Now take your first letter of this string and using the 🔪 method, which can give us the part we need. Its signature is:

🐖 🔪 from 🚂 length 🚂 ➡ 🔤

This will tell us that the 🔪 method can take two arguments that have been named **from** and **length**, both should be of the type 🚂. 🚂 represents an integer, and that this method returns the instance that is needed and is 🔤.

Now call it within the string that we are working on currently:

🐖 🐮 ➡ 🔤 🍇

🔪 🐕 0 1

🍉

This gets our string that contains our first characters of that string and is represented by 🐏. You can then compare 🐏 to **this** or to **self** in many other languages. However, we must store these results somewhere else.

The above code helps store this result within the variable **firstLetter**. The variable is then actually declared and also initialized here. You should notice that 🍦 was used within the code to declare the variables that are preventing the variables from being changed within. These are called the "frozen variable."

We didn't declare the type for this variable either. Emojicode can support type which can create inference within this compiler that infers that the variables are assigned by type and are being looked at for the type of the value for the whole variable.

Now we need to get the rest of the word.

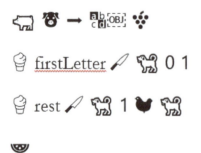

Within this string we start with the  method and then it returns with the length of the string, so we can get the whole string. You can see that the result of this 🐔 method is also used as an argument to 🔪 .

Lastly, we will just need to do a concatenate of the **firstLetter**, rest, and ay, and then return to it from the method.

🛖 🐖 → 🔤 ✲

🍦 firstLetter 🖊 🐕 0 1

🍦 rest 🖊 🐕 1 🐔 🐕

🍎 🍪 rest firstLetter ᴬᵇ𝒸ay ᴬᵇ𝒸 🍪

🍉

The 🍪s is the best option and the most effective way for you to concatenate strings. You can wrap any number of strings between the 🍪 and concatenate them into a string. You should, at this time, already know the 🍎 from above. It can return the value within the method.

Awesome work! Let's update this 🏁 method to give us a few examples similar to the example below. Your file should now at this point look like this example:

🐢 🔤 ✲

🛖 🐖 → 🔤 ✲

🍦 firstLetter 🖊 🐕 0 1

105

```
🍦 rest 🔪 🐕 1 🍗 🐕

🍎 🍪 rest firstLetter 🔤ay🔤 🍪

🍉

🍉

🏁 🍇

😀 🐷 🔤cat🔤

😀 🐷 🔤development🔤

😀 🐷 🔤computer🔤

🍉
```

Compiled you will see:

```
emojicodec greeter.emojic
emojicode greeter.emojib
atcay
evelopmentday
omputercay
```

Chapter Twenty
Creating a Game

To create a game, we need to first import an allegro package into the system.

allegro⬤

This will create all the types from within the allegro package that is available in the namespace ⬤.

Now we should use the startup application, this will help us create the 🏁 function:

 app △

In the 🏁 function, you can see, that there is already some code. 🌀 is one of the types of method calls. This can mean that we call this a method 🖐 directly on top of the type 🔺. Then there is a block code. This code block will create a closure which takes an argument app of the type 🔺. The closures can become a function which, when captured in the context with which it was created, the variables with the objects for the method was called.

The 🖐 type of method within the 🔺 class, which can be provided by the allegro package, this is really an important part that initiates the application in which such a way can be displayed with windows and then you receive the events and the sound that plays during the game. This method would normally not return but instead, it calls the given callable within the appropriate parameters and then passes it through an instance of which will represent what you created in the application. In a moment it will be used to draw the images. We'll use it to draw in a moment.

To recap: Call this type of method, and then provide it with the callable and begin the setup of the application from there.

The next steps are to do so by creating an instance. An instance is what is responsible for displaying your graphics on the computer's screen. On many of the operating systems, a will be the representation of a window.

provides a single initializer:

width height

The code that gets the display begins with:

display 1000 1000

Next, we want to use the instance so that we can configure the programming.

dispay Cookie Monster Game

This is a good time to test to see if everything is working good so far. With this code, we know that it is simply going to load and then immediately terminate. So, instead of running it with a terminate, we must add a few seconds before it closes out. We do that by adding in this code.

😀🕥📛 10_000_000

The 🕥 will make the program wait for some microseconds to terminate. This is typed in as 10,000,000 which is equivalent to 10 seconds. Now, save that file and compile it so that it will run. The image may look like this one below.

Now let's make some cookies to appear on the screen. Download a cookie image and then copy it into your directory so that you can store it in your program. You will have to load it as a bitmap in order for it to display on the screen. There is a 🖼️ within the bitmap class that will initialize this exact step. It's called 📄 and it takes the path to the image that it has been declared for.

You should have noted the 🔊 ☁️. This will indicate that the initializer might have a return with an error that is instead a bitmap object which indicates that the initializer might return an error instead of a bitmap object. We should deal with the error and assume that it will never occur again.

The  will tell us that the compiler with which we use is sure that there will never be errors.

Now that the bitmap is set up we can draw it out on the screen:

```
🎨 app ◇🎨🆕 255 255 255 255
📼 app cookieBmp 500 500
🎬 app
```

Make sure you place this code *prior to* 🍪🗨🪒 10_000_000 or you won't see anything. If everything goes as planned, you should be able to see a tasty cookie on the front of a white background. This should be neatly centered in the display.

The 🎨 method type will fill the entire target drawing while giving them the color which was created for providing the RGBA values. The 📼 method will then draw a bitmap within the specified coordinates. Finally, the 🎬 method makes all the changes visible. Included is everything you have drawn with the back buffer first and then they get visible once you use the 🎬 method.

Now we extend the code even further to show the cookie monster and the cookies.

```
🖥 allegro 🔴
🏁 🐚
  🍪🔺 🐚 app 🔺
    🔾 display ◇🖥🔲 1000 1000
    🎨 display ➖Cookie Monster Game➖

    🔾 cookieBmp 🔵◇🖼📄 ➖cookie.png➖
    🎨 app ◇🎨🔲 255 255 255 255
    📼 app cookieBmp 500 500
    📼 app cookieBmp 400 400 🍪 The Cookie Monster can never get enough cookies

    🔾 monster 🔵◇🖼📄 ➖cookie_monster.png➖
    📼 app monster 200 200

    🎬 app

    🍪🗨🪒 10_000_000
  🍪🍪
```

This should run and display something like the image below.

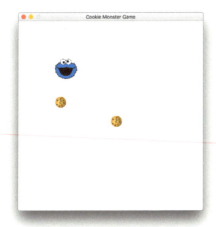

Next, we create a class.

We shall create a class which shall represent the Cookie Monster.

```
🏠 🦉 🐌
   🏠 x 🔌
   🏠 y 🔌
   🏠 monster 🖼

🐴 ▪ 🐌
     🍶 x 500
     🍶 y 500
     🍶 monster ⬛◆🖾☐ ⬛cookie_monster.png⬛
   🍉

🐴 ✏ app △ 🐌
     ⬛ app monster x y
   🍉
🍉
```

Then we create the cookie class.

Then we update the function to use these classes.

Now you will see something like this.

Now we need to make the event a queue that will allow the cookie monster to move.

Then we need to *run* a *loop*.

Next, we set the key down event and determine which ways the cookie monster can move.

We must determine the keycode that will move them left, right, up, down, and then connect it to the :

The last step is to redraw the characters within the loop so that it runs effectively.

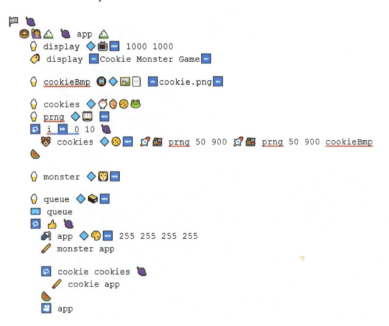

Me want eat cookies!

Now we need to add two methods to the game so that cookie monster can eat them:

We now replace the ⚫'s ✏ method with a much more advanced method:

Now we need to update the loop so that it draws cookies.

```
🔦 iterator 🔷🍴🍪🔘🆕 cookies
🔢 cookie iterator 🐚
🍎 🔪 🕹cookie app 👉 monster 🔱 monster 🐚
   🔄 iterator
🍂
```

Now run your game and enjoy eating cookies with the cookie monster.

Keeping Score

You must download a font file and place it in the *cookie.emojic* file directory. This will help you to keep score. Keeping score is a great way to make your game even more fun. You can find fonts on dafont.com or google fonts. You must load that font into the loop.

```
🔦 font 📱🔷🎲📄 🔠Monoton-Regular.ttf🔠 63
```

Make sure you check for errors. You do not want to get all the way to the end and have no ability to keep score. So, no matter what, throughout the whole process of designing your game, you want to check and double check to ensure that the all of your code is correct and working.

In the run loop, you will want to draw a number of cookies that are left over after the cookie monster has eaten them.

```
🈁 app font 🈁 🎨 cookies 10 990 10 🔷⚖️🆕 🔷🍪🆕 0 0 0 255
```

When you place this code within the game program using the 🎭 *app.* ᵃᵇ꜀ᵈ will draw the text that it is using within the given font. You can define this as the code shows below.

```
🔒 🐖 🈁 font 🎲 text 🈁 x 🎨 y 🎨 align ⚖️ color 🥧 🆒 ✨
```

116

Now you must test the game and check to see if there is a counter at the top of the screen. It should be able to count down the number of cookies that he has eaten and the number of cookies that are left to eat.

Now that we have the cookies, the monster, the music, the text, and the scorecard, we will need an end of the game page. This page will tell us that the game is over.

This new loop must be placed around the loop that is placed around the cookies and prior to the new events that will be taking place. Once you have collected all the cookies you will see this screen.

The Acoustic Experience

Now we will need some great sound for the game. This is essential for games since most people will recognize the theme song to just about anything. You must grab a sound bite from a royalty free sound cloud system. And then you must place them in the *cookie.emojic* file. The *sound.wav* can play when you are inside the cookie monster game and also when cookie monster eats a cookie. Then we should run it through the run loop.

```
🎙 sample 🔘◆🎵📄 🔊sound.wav◀
```

The next step is to add some code that will allow the sound to play after the cookie has been eaten.

```
🔁 cookie iterator 🍪
  🔴 🖌 🍵cookie app 👉 monster 🎙 monster 🍪
    ⓧ iterator
  🔴 ▶ 🐥 cookies 0 🍪
    🏳 sample 1 0 1
  🍉
 🍉
🍉
```

A little bit of explanation is needed for this one. There is a method that can be written to apply sound at the right moment in the game. It also helps to control the volume. When the well-done screen pops up, you can include the sound_end.wav, and mention in the code, when the sound should be played.

```
🎙 endSample 🔘◆🎵📄 🔊sound_end.wav◀
🏳 endSample 1 0 1
```

Now you should have the whole entire code for this program worked out. The code for this program has been placed in the images below. This is the whole code all placed together so that you can see how it will all come together with each section laid out perfectly.

Your whole code for the program should now resemble this one below.

```
🐁 ⊗ 🐋
🏠 cookie 🖼
🏠 x ✏️
🏠 y ✏️

🍴 🔠 🄰 x ✏️ 🄰 y ✏️ 🄰 cookie 🖼 🐋🍎

🐖 🖊 app 🔺 monsterX ✏️ monsterY ✏️ 🔠 🔥 🐋
  🍎 🍥🍴🔠 monsterX x 🔠 monsterX ➕ x 50 🍥🔠 monsterX y 🔠 monsterY ➕
y 50 🐋
    🍎 👍
  🍉
    📺 app cookie x y
    🐋 🔻
  🍉
🍉

🚩 🐋
  ⭕🐁🔺 🐋 app 🔺
  👇 display 🍥📱🔠 1000 1000
  🍊 display 🔠Cookie Monster Game🔠

  👇 cookieBmp 🔘🍥🖼📄 🔠cookie.png🔠

  👇 cookies 🍥🍪🍴🐋
  👇 prng 🍥💻 🔠
  ✏️ i 🔠 0 10 🐋
    🐻 cookies 🍥⊗🔠 ✏️🎲 prng 50 900 ✏️🎲 prng 50 900 cookieBmp
  🍉

  👇 sample 🔘🍥🎵📄 🔠sound.wav🔠

  👇 font 🔘🍥🅰📄 🔠Monoton-Regular.ttf🔠 63
  👇 monster 🍥🗾🔠

  👇 queue 🍥🎒🔠
  📺 queue
  🎲 🍎 🐋
    🔫 app 🍥🎮🔠 255 255 255 255
    🖊 monster app

    👇 iterator 🍥🍯🍴⊗🔠 cookies
```

Well done! Now you can enjoy your very own Emojicode Game.

Now that I have given you a step by step process for not only designing a program but also a step by step for designing a game, you should be well on your way to using Emojicode. Emojicode is for everyone. It is so simple your child can do it efficiently and with ease. All it takes is a bit of know-how and the time to sit down and type out all that code. So, now that you have read all the way through this book, you should have a better grasp on what Emojicode is, how it can be used, and steps to take to ensure that you use it in a purposeful and effective manner.

The next time you are looking for something to do for fun or want to create a ridiculously fun game, you can come back to this book and use it as a reference source for creating whatever it is that you wish to design.

Glossary

Emojicode - is a form of computer programming that allows the programmer to designate a form of language that is represented by emojis.

Optionals - "there is a value, and it equals x" or "there isn't a value at all." A variable that can have a nil. When you use this value, you need to unwrap it.

Absence of value - nil is used to mean the number zero.

Closures - blocks full of code that is immediately executable, but they maintain the context in which they were created. The variables and the method context can be passed around the program.

Generics - will allow you to write some of the code in which you can use a placeholder, such as variable names, instead of the actual name type, which can then be substituted with a real type that is available when you use the source code later.

List of texts – a tool that is used to help store several pieces of information all at once.

Compiler - computer software that can transform the code written from a certain programming language into another programming language.

Execution Engine - a process by which the computer or virtual machine can perform a simple set of instructions for the computer program. These instructions will trigger sequences of simple actions on the executable machine.

Boolean - a binary variable, having two possible values called "true" and "false."

Meta types - used to define the postfix notation, different types of web pages, HTML tags, and related words which have been denoted by meta identifiers.

Metadata - data that is about data. This will include production time, origin, and format.

Memory Management – the process of controlling and then coordinating computer memory. This assigns portions that are called blocks for various running programs in order to optimize the overall system performance. This will reside in the hardware and the OS as well as in the programs and applications.

OS - Operating System.

Garbage collection - this is a form of automatic memory management. This will attempt to reclaim the garbage, or memory that is being occupied by objects that are not in use within the program.

Callable - any object which can be called like a function.

Namespaces - an abstract container, as well as environment, created to hold a logical grouping of the unique identifier or symbols. The identifier is defined within the namespace that is associated with only that namespace.

Error Handling - this process is comprised of anticipation, detection, and resolution of applicable errors, programming errors as well as communication errors. The error handling will help in maintaining the normal flow of the program's executable steps.

Initializer - the assignment of an initial value for data objects or variable. The manner can be initialized by performing the programming language, as well as types of storage class, that is within the object that is initialized.

Perfect Extraction - this is the act of retrieving data that is coming from data sources which are further pulled from a data processor or data storage system.

Types - are a clarification of data that tells the compiler how the programmers would intend to use the data. These can be real, Boolean, or integers.

Enumerations - the data type that consists of a set of named values which can be considered members, elements, enumeral, or enumerators within the types set.

Protocols - this is considered an interface which is a common means in order for unrelated objects to have communication within them. They can define values as well as methods within the objects that will agree upon the order to cooperate.

Inheritance - this will enable the new objects to take on a few properties of the existing objects. The class that is used for the basis of the inheritance is named a superclass or base class. This will inherit from the superclass which is named the subclass or derived class.

Overriding - the language that features a subclass or child class which can provide a specific implementation within the method that is already provided within one of its superclass or parent class.

Unwrapping - to get the value of the variable in order to use it.

Nothingness test - this is the test in which we test for null. The absence of something.

Condition Assignment - these are the features of a programming language that performs a separate computation that depends on whether a programmer is specified with Booleans conditions which are evaluations of the truth or false of it.

Class - this is a template definition that defines the method s and variable s within a particular kind of set objects. The object is specific in its instance of a class, and it contains the real values instead of the variables. The class will be the one that is defining the ideas of object-oriented programming.

Value type - within the computer programming genre the coded object will involve the memory allocation that is directly where it was created. These can be commonly contrasted in order to reference the types that act instead as a pointer to a value which is stored in another location.

Methods - this is the programmed procedure which is able to be defined as a part of the class and includes any number of objects within that class. Classes can be more than one method.

Deprecation - is a language entity which will be tolerated or supported, however, is not recommended. The number of elements and attributes are deprecated within the HTML 4.0, and the meaning that other means can be accomplished within the task as preferred.

Identity Check - object-oriented designs within the object-oriented analysis that describes him the property of objects that will distinguish them from the other objects.

Instantiation - to create an instance, for example, to define one variation of the object that is within the class. This gives it a name, as well as a location that is in this physical place. Some writers say that you may instantiate the class of an object that is created and a concrete instance of the class.

Reserved Emojis - these would be emojis that are reserved due to the terms or phrases which are appropriate for a special use and they may not be able to be utilized in the creation of the variable names.

Native Binaries - this is the language that is understood by the computer. Binary is understood as the language within the computer. Native is the code that can be written to run on a specific processor.

Mutability - Immutable objects are those that cannot be modified after they are created. Mutability simply put means that these objects can be modified once they are created.

Lists - this tool is something that can be stored within multiple pieces of information at one given time. This can also be defined as a variable that contains multiple instances of variables. This can consist of numbers which are paired with items. All the items can be retrieved by its numbered pair.

String pooling - this is a pool of strings that will heap memory together. The string is a special class that is assigned in the programmer's system and we can create a string object by using the new operators and providing values in double quotes.

S Package – a namespace that is organized in a set of relatable classes and interfaces. You can conceptually think of the packages in a similar function within the different folders of your computer. This might be using HTML pages in one folder, the images in another, and then the scripts and applications within another.

Control flow - this is the order in which the individual statements and instructions can function within calls that are imperative to the program being executed or even evaluated.

Syntax - this refers to any rules that have specified the correct sequences of combined symbols which can be used in the form of a program that is correctly structured in any given programming language.

Literals - the program that is written exactly as it should be to be interpreted properly.

Scoping variables - the name that can represent the different values that are executed during the program.

Comments - this is a programmer's explanation that is readable and annotated in the code for the source of a computer program. They can be added with the purpose of creating the source code easier for the humans to be able to understand and are generally ignored by the compilers and the interpreters.

Deinitialization - called right before the class in deallocated within the instance. You must write this with the deinit keyword. This is similar to how to initialize is wrote in the init keyword. They are only available within the class type.

Arch Linux - composed of free and open source software predominantly, and then supports the involvement of the community. They have a comprehensive documentation in which the form of the community Archwiki is known.

Package API - API-application programming interface. This is a set of the subroutine definitions, tools for building the software, and communication protocols. Those listed here; POSIX, Windows API, and ASPI are all examples of these types of API. These are usually able to facilitate the use of implementation.

IBus - Intelligent Input Bus or IBus is a framework for multilingual inputs within the Unix-like operating systems.

Hex Code - this is a way to specifically identify the code or hexadecimal of a color, value, or level of a component. This will usually start with a # and can then be followed by 6 values or 3 pairs of values.

Conclusion

Thank you for purchasing this book.

I hope this book was an informative and interesting read for you. Programming on Emojicode is a great hobby to develop since you can write small programs and design games as well.

The Emojicode Programming book for Parents is a great way to understand the language. Over the course of the book, you will gather information on how the Emojicode was developed, how to code, and how to build your first game. The book will help you every step of the way.

The next step is to enjoy this book as much as I have enjoyed writing it for you and remember that with each new day we have the opportunity to learn something new. So, why not learn how to program in Emojicode?

www.ingramcontent.com/pod-product-compliance
Lightning Source LLC
LaVergne TN
LVHW072049060326
832903LV00053B/301